Saloons
of
San Francisco

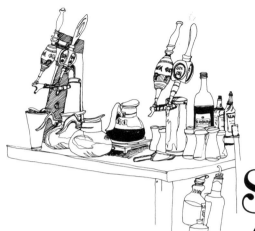

Saloons of San Francisco

The Great and Notorious

Jane Chamberlin

Text by
Hank Armstrong

Introduction Research
Dustin F. Leer

CAPRA PRESS / 1982

Santa Barbara

Cover and page design by Marcia Burtt.
Map treatment by Alex Marshall.
Camerawork by Earl Deyer.
Typesetting by McAdams Type.
Printed by Fairfield Graphics.

Library of Congress Cataloging in Publication Data

Chamberlin, Jane, 1931-
    The great and notorious Saloons of
San Francisco.

    1. Chamberlin, Jane, 1931-   . 2. San
Francisco (Calif.) —Bars, saloons, etc.—
Pictorial works. 3. Hotels, taverns, etc.,
in art. I. Armstrong, Hank, 1945-
II. Title.
NC139.C45A4   1982   917.94'610453   82-12763
ISBN 0-88496-186-9

CAPRA PRESS
Post Office Box 2068
Santa Barbara, California 93120

Contents

Introduction 7
Foreword 15
Map 16

NORTH BEACH
Vesuvio Cafe 18
Albatross Saloon 20
Spec's Twelve Adler 22
The Tosca 24
Enrico's 26
The Saloon 28
Lost & Found 30
Savoy Tivoli 32
Gino & Carlo 34
New Pisa 36
Washington Square Bar & Grill 38

DOWNTOWN
Cookie's Star Buffet 40
Red's Place 42
Paoli's 44
Harrington's 46
Schroeder's 48
Templebar 50
Hoffman's Grill 52
House of Shields 54
Happy Valley Bar 56
Redwood Room 58
Top of the Mark 60
Kimball's 62

WATERFRONT
Buena Vista 64
Eagle Cafe 66
Pier 23 68
Bouncer's 70
Mission Rock Resort 72

CASTRO/NOE VALLEY
Twin Peaks Tavern 74
Finnegan's Wake 76

SUNSET DISTRICT
Lost Weekend 78
Beach Chalet 80
Cliff House 82
Maud's 84
The Anxious Asp 86

CLEMENT STREET
Churchill's 88
Holy City Zoo 90
The Plough & The Stars 92

UNION/CHESTNUT/POLK
Liverpool Lil's 94
Paul's Saloon 96
The Chestnut Street Grill 98
Pierce St. Annex 100
Balboa Cafe 102
Perry's 104
Henry's Africa 106
Buzzby's 108

MISSION DISTRICT
Hotel Utah 110
Stud 112
Hamburger Mary's 114
Swede's 116
Rainbow Cattle Co. 118
La Rondalla 120
Bajone's 122
Old Homestead 124

ARMY STREET
Old Clam House 126

Acknowledgments 128

Introduction

WHOEVER WRITES the definitive history of San Francisco ought to write it under dim light, with both elbows propped on a well-worn bar, a sheaf of cocktail napkins for stationery and a bottle of Anchor Steam beer for good company.

This city's history deserves that.

After all, as much of it seems to have taken place between the walls of saloons as outside them. In fact, the city came into the world in one. In 1844, surveyor Jean Jacques Vioget's map of the backwater hamlet of Yerba Buena resided under the tender care of one Englishman by the name of Robert Ridley. Ridley's billiard room and saloon, incidentally, happened to serve as the town social center as well. (Some things in life don't change.) Anyone who wished to buy a large lot in soon-to-be downtown San Francisco merely paid the Alcalde (mayor) a few dollars. Ridley then dutifully inserted the name on the proper plot on the map. To seal the deal, the new owner was obliged to buy a few horns of the local moonshine for all present.

In 1846, Captain John Montgomery and company from the warship U.S.S. Portsmouth landed on shore, raised the American flag, and officially relieved Mexico of any further responsibility for the area. And two years following, with James Marshall's discovery of gold, the city became an instant reality.

San Francisco, city by the Golden Gate; built by gold in a turbulent fever of work and emotions, not the least of which was greed. It proved for some a Sodom and Gomorroh, for others an economic Holy Land, and for most, a tempestuous, uneasy alliance between the two.

Population of the child-city, San Francisco of the 1850s, swelled almost exclusively with men, abandoning a sea of ships clogging the harbor, drinking and brawling and gambling and spending and whoring when they could, and not giving a sweet damn if the outside world was scandalized.

The hills were bursting with gold. Whatever could be had and lost could be had again. When one New York Evening Post correspondent ranted and raved that "The people of San Francisco are mad, stark mad!" his shout blew away unheeded in the winds of opportunity enveloping the town. That madness filled a city, pulling men from the four corners of the earth as a magnet pulls iron filings.

In little more than a year, from 1849 to 1850, the population grew from several hundred to more than twenty-five thousand, most of it living in leaky tents and shanties.

For a time, reality outran imagination at every turn. Space proved so limited that rocking chairs and coffins were sought-after sleeping quarters, and men paid good money for one. At one point in 1848, a pound of gold bought a pound of tacks, and a gallon of whiskey went for one hundred dollars.

Saloons were the chief beneficiaries of the good fortune, and they proliferated. The famed El Dorado saloon, across whose tables a quarter of a million dollars a day passed, was at its start a fifteen-by-twenty-five foot canvas tent on Portsmouth Square, commanding forty thousand dollars a year in rent. Lots that the Alcalde dispensed for a few dollars suddenly went for tens of thousands of dollars after the rush started.

About the same time Mme. Simone Jules, a beautiful Frenchwoman, made her entrance at the Bella Vista and became the first female croupier, Ed Moses walked into a rival's gambling house and lost two hundred thousand dollars in a single sitting, and one drunken miner risked twenty thousand dollars on a single turn of a card.

A bleak expanse of sand passed for Portsmouth Square, but around it, saloons like the Parker House and Dennison's Exchange did a boomtown business. Women were as rare a sight as an elephant for a time, and children more so. When a woman did walk the streets, she drew respectful crowds of painfully-chivalrous miners before and aft.

And while gold sat heaped in piles on tables everywhere,

mingling as payment with coins from all over the world, the streets outside at times turned to morasses of mud so deep as to swallow whole wagons, team and all. Horses and mules, and, rumor persisted, even men, had drowned in the streets.

Six times in a span of two years the city burned to the ground, or a good part of it, at least a couple of those times at the hands of rowdies from the burgeoning slum of Sydney Town on the slopes of Telegraph Hill. But what goes down must come up, and the city did, with a vengeance, each time.

Sydney Town, the precursor of the infamous Barbary Coast; its dens were sordid little affairs, the price of entry sometimes being life and limb. They bore names like the Noggin of Ale and The Bird-In-Hand, the Tam O'-Shanter and the Jolly Waterman. Their denizens were men like Dirty Tom Maclear, who for a few cents willingly ate or drank any refuse thrown his way.

The Boar's Head offered a woman and a boar engaged in highly questionable acts, while the Fierce Grizzly lived up to its moniker by chaining a live female grizzly just inside its door.

San Francisco, the instant city, with neither memories nor tradition to hinder it. By and large, the strong and quick came out on top, and men made their own laws at the price of a politician or two. Drinking and gambling were the salt and pepper of city life, and wenching, when the harlots began to arrive in droves, the sugar. Supplies might be traded pound-for-pound for gold, but a woman could cost a man's fortune for a time. A kiss went for three ounces of gold, full service for four pounds of it.

A man had a choice of three kinds of saloons in the 1850s; high class, low class and miserable. By 1851, San Francisco was importing seven bottles of champagne for every one consumed in Boston. In 1860, the city possessed more than eight hundred groggeries and an average murder rate of almost two a day over years when its population never topped forty thousand. In 1870, twenty thousand barrels of whiskey, two thousand barrels of brandy and two hundred thousand cases of wine were imported to fuel the boom.

As years went by, the rich kept getting richer, and drunk, while the poor just kept getting drunk. While the wealthy frequented the magnificent Palace Hotel when it was built, and fancy French restaurants that went up in the later 1800s, the Barbary Coast thrived in all its danger and alluring wickedness. Gentlefolk like Shanghai Kelly, Liverpool Lil and Miss Piggott gainfully employed themselves in the shanghai trade. While Kelly preferred the three trap doors that lined the front of his bar, he wasn't above the occasional usage of a bungstarter. Mickey Finns, opium-soaked cigars, laudanum and Miss Piggott's axe handle all served to provide an unannounced tour of duty at sea.

The 1890s ushered in the "Champagne Era" and its "Cocktail Route" in full force. Each day, a goodly crowd struck out after work for the circuit, wending their way down Market, up Kearney to Sutter and over to Powell. Nellie Coit, whose tribute to firemen was firehose-shaped Coit Tower, took to washing her hair in champagne.

Herb Caen once noted an old clip from the Oakland "Daily Transcript" of the day remarking dryly that "The police of San Francisco arrested four hundred and eighty-eight drunks last month, only eight of which were 'common' ones. Drunks in that town are generally of a remarkable character." Danger and depravity mingled with light and mirth.

Something rare lived in those times. A magic of a kind, when an entire city turned a fond eye toward foibles and frivolity. Some of the most famous and most pampered characters of the time sported names like George Washington Coombs, "the Great Matrimonial Candidate," Old Rosey, Money King and the Great Unknown. Oofty-Goofty, "The Man Who Knew No Pain" (in one part of his anatomy anyway) solicited people in saloons to hit him with a baseball bat for a modest fee. Unfortunately for Oofty, one good swing from "The

Great John L.," boxer John L. Sullivan, sent Oofty sprawling unconscious. When he awoke, Oofty discovered that Sullivan's blow had restored his ability to feel pain.

But the greatest eccentric in a city enamored of eccentricity bore the name Emperor Norton, the self-proclaimed Emperor of the United States. Grandly uniformed and given to issuing proclamations about his non-existent empire, he paid his way about town with handwritten script happily accepted almost everywhere.

Then the city that gave little thought to tomorrow suddenly came to ruin. April 18, 1906 brought the earthquake and fire that left the city devastated with four hundred million dollars in damage and four square miles destroyed by fire. Out of the ruins emerged stories worthy of the city; two young ladies, a bottle of whiskey and a salvaged piano planted in Jefferson Square, the ladies singing to the world "There'll be A Hot Time in the Old Town Tonight" while the city burned; and Hotaling and Company, repository for the largest stock of whiskey on the West Coast, rose tall, proud and distinctly untouched among the wreckage of churches, public buildings and other more virtuous edifices around it. That miracle of sorts prompted Charlie Field's verse

"If, as they say God spanked
The town for being over-frisky,
Why did he burn the churches down
And spare Hotaling's whiskey?"

Frisky; like Frisco, a nickname for the city-before-the-quake that a few people had begun to grumble self-consciously about before disaster struck. It seemed, well, too frivolous, just too undignified for such a grand old city. Its people loved it with an intensity equaled only perhaps by New York's, and now it was gone, a mirage.

Hotaling's good fortune insured that the saloons opened again expeditiously, which they did en masse of course. And the new Palace Hotel nearly matched the old in grandeur, but the Barbary Coast had been dealt a mortal blow, and its successor more or less, the Tenderloin, catered to the rich, and never matched the Barbary Coast's glory. The city to come might prove bigger and even greater, but it could never prove the same. And suddenly, burned into the collective brain, was a painful awareness of the biggest memory of all: 1906.

Now, memories of this century abound. Memories of a wild and woolly Prohibition where speedboats supplied the speakeasies which sprouted about town, one of the best operating directly across the street from the Old Hall of Justice. Officials managed to look the other way more or less, as long as they got their graft on time. Memories of the "percentage girls," who first danced for pay and later provided a bit more, and of faces like Little Egypt's, a winsome Night Dancer who plied her trade at the Poulet D'Or, known to most as the Poodle Dog, and at Spider Kelly's in the years following the quake. Pacific Street was "Terrific Street" in the early 1900s, until Broadway eventually supplanted it as the nocturnal oasis.

The Bohemian Club, founded before the turn of the century, counted among its membership such luminaries as Ambrose Bierce, Jack London and George Sterling. Originally congregating in the Astor House on the Montgomery Block, they were driven out by the businessmen so they found refuge in places like Luna's and Poppa Coppa's on the edge of the International Settlement, the precursor to North Beach.

During Prohibition, they could be found drinking grappa at Izzy Gomez's. Izzy was a three-hundred-pound, bullet-headed piece of humanity purported to have been a master at the shanghai trade. In their philosophy were the seeds of the beatnik rebellion nurtured in North Beach.

World War II brought the servicemen in force, and the arrival of "B girls," strip joints and prostitutes on Broadway and elsewhere. In 1950s San Francisco, incongruity prevailed, as always. While North Beach spawned Kerouac and the Beat Generation in places like Henry Lenoir's 12 Adler Cafe, Vesuvio and Gino and Carlo, the social scenes of the city were played out in the Clift Hotel's Redwood Room and the Palace Hotel.

We always love just a little more what we are about to lose, or what we have loved and lost. San Francisco falters today in middle age, afflicted by mirrored corporate monoliths built on some fabled ruins. The new face is lifted from the old, and the lift is up, for worse, not better. But that kernel of the city laid out in Ridley's saloon 125-odd years ago still lays out around Portsmouth Square today.

The city born in a saloon still thrives on them, but memories of the past play on the uncertainty of the future. Mr. San Francisco may not be too sure what to do about it, or even what he did wrong, let alone where his city goes from here. Maybe he thinks about it over a martini at the House of Shields, or a beer at Specs', or an Irish at the beloved Buena Vista. And maybe he gives way to his frustration briefly, then says "Thank God this joint's still here, anyway." We lost the City of Paris, sure enough, but we saved Hoffman's. Didn't we?

For every saloon in this town remembered, maybe ten, maybe a hundred have come and gone. They stay briefly or longer, and when they leave, linger for a time like ghosts in the memories of their displaced patrons, until they slip away without a trace most of the time. From the outset, San Francisco staked its claim as the greatest drinking city in the world, a title it shows no interest in relinquishing.

At any moment, better than any historian could, the saloons of the city can show where its heart and soul have been, and where they're headed. A hundred years old or a day, they stand as living museums where the oral tradition survives lustily.

This book will not tell you how to drink, or even where. And if it succeeds, it will tell less about the bars themselves than the people who fill them. The path between the Stud, say, and the Happy Valley in the Palace Hotel will not prove a beaten one, but a few in search of the city will tread it out of curiosity.

So, in these drawings and these words, we celebrate the watering holes of San Francisco, but more importantly, we celebrate the people who bring them to life. People like Enrico Banducci, rampantly Italian, made of fire and ice, enraptured while his young daughter turns tentative pliés in the middle of his restaurant, or the flamboyant Norm Hobday of Henry Africa's, an odd man on his most even days, or the sound of the staccato beat pounded out from the hard heels of step dancers at the Plough and Stars, or even the foundry worker at the Old Homestead in the Mission, out of work but still buying a round for a writer out of pride, when it never happened at a "nicer" place.

Saloons breed memories, fair and foul, as quiet as the desultory clink of ice against glass and as wild as dance with maracas and tambourines on a warm summer night. They are the most human of all creations.

The city may grow old gracefully, in doubt as that may seem at the moment. Or the next well-timed roll of a dice cup may prove the one to bring the town crashing down again. Either way, to the end, bars will remain the threads in the social fabric of the City By The Bay.

So a toast to the city that was; to a beauty all the more haunting somehow when seen from the corner of the eye; to the spirit to build well and build again if need be, to the willingness "to match destiny for beers," and most of all to a wild and unkempt city that forever strives for immortality, knowing it can never have it, and never giving up.

14

Foreword

I almost think I have been the *accoucheur* of Chamberlin's book on Great and Notorious Saloons of San Francisco. I remember seeing her with pens and paper around various saloons in the North Beach area. I got to know her slightly, and discovered that she had a genuine interest in the life of the inside of a saloon, though she never appeared to take a drink. I think her book of drawings is absolutely first-rate and catches the curious loneliness and anomie of the sole drinker in the saloon. Her best drawings seem to me about single drinkers. Her text by Hank Armstrong matches her sympathy to this strange and comforting kind of life. I heartily recommend the book to drinkers and non-drinkers.

—CHARLES MCCABE

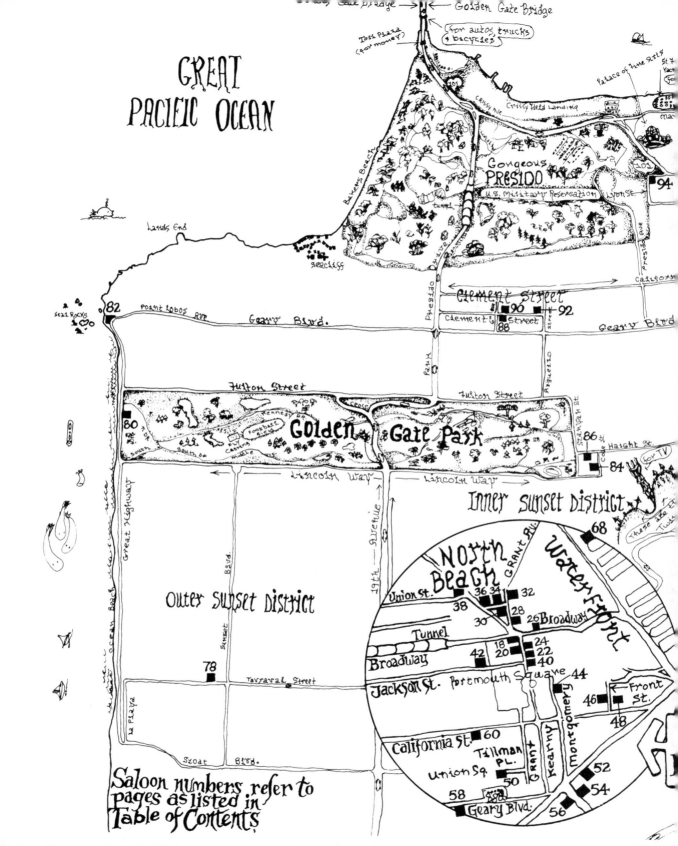

GREAT
PACIFIC OCEAN

Golden Gate Bridge

Toll Plaza
(for money)

(for autos, trucks
& bicycles)

Palace of Fine Arts

Crissy Ave   Crissy Field Landing

Gorgeous
PRESIDO
U.S. Military Reservation   Lyons St.

94

Lands End

Sea Cliffs

Clement Street

Point Lobos Ave   Geary Blvd.

Clement   Street   92

Clement   Street   90

88

Geary Blvd

82

Seal Rocks

Fulton Street

Fulton Street

80

Kennedy Dr.
Football field
Casting

Golden   Gate Park

86   Cole Haight St.

84   for TV

Lincoln Way   Lincoln Way

Inner Sunset District

Great Highway

Sunset Blvd.

Outer Sunset District

19th Avenue

these are
Twin

68

North
Beach

Waterfront

Union St.   36 34   32
38   28
30   26 Broadway
Tunnel
Broadway   18   24
42   20   22
40
Jackson St. Portsmouth Square   44

46   Front St.

48

California St.   60

Tillman
PL.

Union Sq

52
54

56

50   58

Geary Blvd.

78

Taraval Street

Sloat   Blvd.

La Playa

Saloon numbers refer to
pages as listed in
Table of Contents

Vesuvio Café

A BALDING CABBIE in his late thirties reminisces loudly about the Weathermen and the Berkeley Days of Rage, while a few punk rockers with neon hair file past to the balcony upstairs and a lone longshoreman pulls at a beer by the window.

Somewhere between the Beat Generation's birth and lin-

18

gering death, Vesuvio Cafe and North Beach bohemianism became one. In the 1950s it became the eye of a creative storm, and its patrons then were fiercely loyal, often brilliant and nearly always rebellious. Kerouac and Ginsberg; Dylan Thomas and Theodore Dreiser; Bob Dylan and Erskine Caldwell; even Robert Oppenheimer and Yehudi Menuhin have found a home here at one time or another.

And in thirty-odd years Vesuvio's has changed little, its clientele still composed largely of artists, writers and North Beach workingfolk. With wild murals outside to challenge the passers-by and an interior that is nothing short of a jumbled work of art, it still personifies North Beach. From its start, the bar has doubled as a gallery for struggling artists and a forum for debate; the alcoholic alter-ego of the City Lights bookstore next door.

The bohemian spirit survives as well, battered and altered a bit by the leaving of the bar's founder and mentor Henri Lenoir in 1969, and by the invasion of North Beach by the topless joints. Vesuvio Cafe still respects creative talent in whatever guise. It is the ultimate in proletarian bars, and that is Lenoir's finest legacy.

255 Columbus Avenue, 362-3370

North Beach • 19

Albatross Saloon

WHEN RODNEY KILGALLON and Sam DuVall rescued this saloon a few years back, they did so in grand style. A bar which had been born as the Andromeda Saloon in 1907, and which subsequently became a mainstay on the Barbary Coast, had been heading inexorably downhill for decades.

Rumors abound about its history, some better founded than others. Jack Dempsey worked the door as bouncer from 1913 to 1914, and, as lore would have it, Baby Face Nelson was captured while playing cards in a backbar stockroom. And if that won't do it, the Andromeda Cafe served alcohol by prescription, "for medicinal purposes only" of course, during Prohibition.

A lot of colorful history and high style in architecture was buried beneath successive coats of paint, a false ceiling, and numerous other ad-hoc redecorations over the years. An eight-month restoration project brought back its elegance and then some, with some fine wood and stained glass craftsmanship its trademark. The long-neglected flame mahogany backbar, built in 1907 expressly for the room, got a facelift. Wood and skylights were exposed, and a new floor of old wood replaced the irreparably worn tile.

Antique punkah wallah fans from Bombay, India, found in the basement at restoration now add a Rube Goldberg touch, revolving desultorily over the bar. And the self-flushing spittoon at the foot of the bar, supposedly used at one time for more than spitting, still remains, thankfully unused.

Pictures and artifacts from the Maritime Museum festoon the walls and, along with various eye-catching antiques, provide the atmosphere.

155 & 159 Columbus Avenue, 434-3344

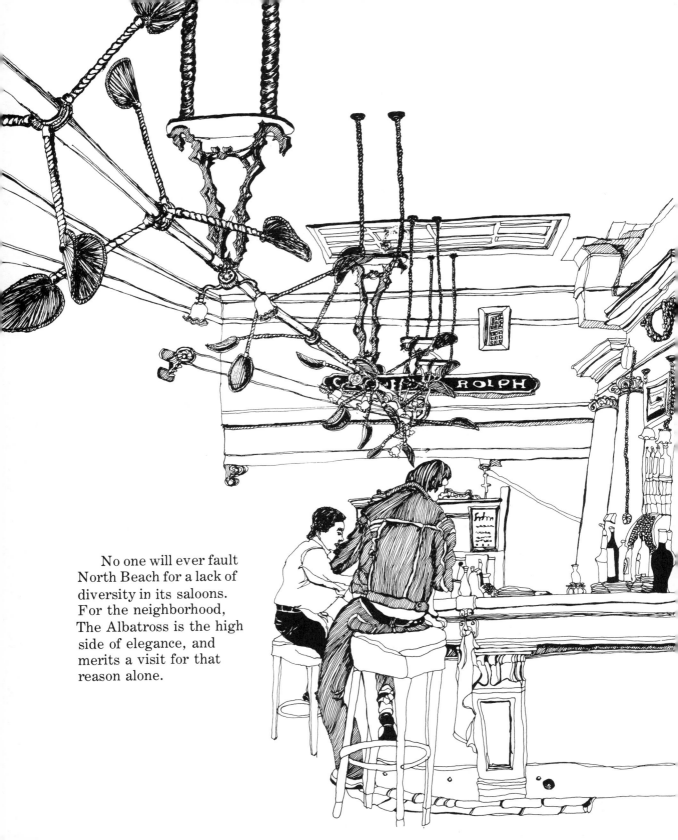

No one will ever fault
North Beach for a lack of
diversity in its saloons.
For the neighborhood,
The Albatross is the high
side of elegance, and
merits a visit for that
reason alone.

Specs' Twelve, Adler

THE SEARCH FOR SPECS' ends in the stub-end of an alley off Columbus, marked mainly by trash and flower boxes, a rough-hewn wooden bench and high-minded graffiti like "Beware the Illuminati" and "Hail AntiChrist." Those who come generally come looking for it. A few fall upon it accidentally, like Alice on the rabbit hole. The rest of the world, fortunately, passes it by unnoticed.

Between the old brick walls of Specs' 12 Adler Museum Cafe is pure, concentrated North Beach. Specs Simmons, ex-sheet metal worker turned bar owner and notable non-philosopher, wields his wit and pragmatism in equal measures to keep order. He ministers to poets and other literati, the few longshoremen and seamen left in the city, to journalists and, of course, the topless dancers from the joint upstairs.

The famous and infamous, the bright and burned out fragments of North Beach expatriotism wander in and out, puzzling the fate of the world and getting drunk. One hundred of them gathered in the middle of Columbus Avenue for a photo once, and it still hangs on the wall.

That photo is not so easy to find, however. Specs' likely never intended the appellation "museum" be taken too seriously (he and his bar don't have a reverent bone in them, unless you count the whale's penis bone hanging over the back bar). Yet it isn't an idle boast. The walls are filled with artifacts; old San Francisco mementos, scrimshaw and sea lore, great clippings and strange signs, and glass cases full of Rabelaisian objects.

Before Specs salvaged the place in the late 60s, it had sported more names and faces than a quick-change artist. Whatever North Beach wanted at the time, and probably a lot it didn't, did time in this little niche on Adler Street. It was variously a haven for Arab music and bellydancing, jazz, lesbians until the owner was busted and the place shut down, and was even a speakeasy during Prohibition. The place once did a stint decked out as a bull ring.

Henri Lenoir, North Beach's spirit incarnate, rescued it briefly in the late 40s. He dubbed it "12 Adler Place" ("street" not appealing to his aesthetics), hung works by local painters on the walls, and the cafe took off. For a time, it was one of the bastions of bohemianism. But that faded, and 12 Adler faded along with it.

Now, the place is enlightened again. Writers and their kind flock to it, while the world-at-large, fortunately, still passes Specs' by.

12 Adler Street, 421-4112

Tosca

EVERY NOCTURNAL JAUNT through the world of North Beach saloons warrants the Tosca at its end. The last stop, after all, is where we bid the evening farewell, a place to contemplate our own excesses in an atmosphere of congenial dignity.

Enter the Tosca. Paintings dark with age capture scenes from Puccini's opera. Two great hissing cauldrons anchor either end of a long bar, dispensing steamed milk for cappucinos with noisy but satisfying fervor, while glasses-at-the-ready line its length. An ancient Cobra model Wurlitzer filled with vintage records of Toscanini, Callas, Pavoratti and other operatic greats competes nowadays with the heavy thud of a disco downstairs. (The basement once housed an indoor bocci court, and with luck, some activity of a similar nature will eventually move back in and leave the Tosca in peace.)

A private backroom once used by the Italian men for cards now houses a pool table for friends of the owners and celebrities who frequent the place. Major renovation struck the Tosca sometime ago when the bathrooms got a new coat of paint, but other than that, little has changed during almost four decades in the same spot. The original Tosca opened in 1919 elsewhere in North Beach.

Tradition dictates that the antique registers, jukebox, and of course cappucino machines must remain. 1939 World's Fair stickers stay untouched on the backbar mirrors. Mario, a white-coated master of the art of tending bar, has ministered here for thirty-five years.

All in all, the Tosca bears no relation to the tawdry indulgences of Broadway nearby. Few tourists are drawn in by the huge neon sign; its patrons are loyal; many began coming with their parents a long time ago in another San Francisco.

On the backbar, fading into its fine wood, hangs a sign that exhorts "Whatever you are, be a good one." The Tosca is.

242 Columbus Avenue, 986-9651 (public telephone)

Enrico's

IF BROADWAY PROMISES nothing else, it promises incongruity. The view from the outdoor tables at Enrico's, such as it is, takes in the "World's Best Male Stripper Cabaret" across the street. Stylishly-dressed people periodically form a line in front of the tables, waiting patiently to get into Finnochio's next door.

The cafe crowd itself is patently North Beach, mingling financial district refugees, people who work the street, lonelies in search of company (especially after 11 p.m.), and a smattering of every other type. Poets and writers abound here, perhaps more so than at any other North Beach haven.

And Enrico Banducci would have it no other way. He dubs his place the "S and S place," sables and sandals fitting comfortably together. The cafe has changed little in more than two decades on Broadway; the waiters are vested, tied and aproned, the walls muralled and hung with gilt-framed mirrors and old photo portraits, and exposed brick coexistent with chandeliers.

There are no dark corners to hide in; no corners at all, in fact. Enrico's passion for round things ("We live in a round world, don't we?" he argues), created an inviting effect. The marble counters and tables, the chairs, the windows, even the front wall, are curved, as if to pull people in from the street.

But the heart and soul of Enrico's is Enrico Banducci himself, a rampantly Italian, omnipresently bereted restaurateur with an abiding love of opera and the classics, the power to charm and infuriate, and no lack of opinions on every subject imaginable.

He arrived in San Francisco at the tender age of fourteen in 1936, and set about making his mark on the city. In 1950, he founded the legendary Hungry i, running it for twenty years until its voluntary demise in 1970. That left him with Enrico's, begun in 1958. Most nights, he still holds court with artistic eccentricity here for friends and strangers.

Despite the invasion of the strip joints, he contends North

Beach has changed little over the years. Enrico's thrives on the incongruous. The only caveat of Enrico Banducci's is "You have to act like a human being. If you don't, you don't have enough money to stay here."

504 Broadway, 392-6220

The Saloon

A FEW LIGHTS THROW a desultory yellow glow into an otherwise mine-like atmosphere, and a few more battered barstools that have to struggle to stay upright on their own seldom have to. The self-flushing spittoon doesn't, hasn't in a long time and is not about to anytime soon; which is just as well, because the crowd at the Saloon might just use it. The backbar from Italy is the most ornate item in the place, but it's old and has settled radically with the years.

In fact, the whole building seems to have screwed itself into the earth in a fit of obstinacy. The city can do what it wants. The Saloon is here to stay.

Having survived 120-odd years in this city doesn't guarantee manners; but character... now, that's a different matter altogether. The Saloon is full of it.

Two staples of the Fresno Hotel made it a pillar of the Barbary Coast—women and booze. So it wasn't exactly random selection coming into play when navy crews enthusiastically hauled their hoses over the hill and spared the bar from the 1906 fire. Priorities will be priorities. For the watering hole, surviving while the rest of the city went down in flames was a typical act of defiance.

Still nearly as rough and blustering as ever, the whole bar has been pulsating of late with some of the best blues in the city. Tourists still grab their children and cross the street to avoid walking by it, which could be a good sign. The place has grown a bit less cantankerous with a cover charge and bouncer. But don't expect miracles. The Saloon is far better off without them.

1232 Grant Avenue, 392-0548

Jane Chamberlin 81 ©

Lost & Found

ON THE SURFACE, it is the Lost and Found, a comfortable, slightly raunchy juke-box-and-pool hole in the Grant Street wall of saloons. A good civilized step up from its bare-knuckled neighbors, the Saloon and Mama Hale's, the Lost and Found is filled and still filling with some fine, off-beat relics. An ancient stop-light here, a barber's chair there, a half boat dredged from the bay and implanted as a bar near the window, a 1952 hummer of a Harley Davidson motorcycle, and a plethora of railroad mementos, each with a good story to tell . . . all in all, an amiable stop on the North Beach odyssey of bars.

Still, there is more. Above the jukebox and chatter are the faint echoes of another saloon that once lived here. A battered wooden sign hanging unobtrusively in one corner declares "Folksinging—Hootenanny Tonight." It is the only relic that survives from the passing of the infamous Coffee Gallery.

The Coffee Gallery was a hotbed of the folk revolution. It was here the Beat Generation coalesced and prospered, nurturing itself with poetry readings, anti-establishment music and the like. It lived and died with bohemianism pretty much, to be replaced by a hard-core blues joint and just recently, the Lost and Found, a good bar in its own right, but even better with the legacy of the Coffee Gallery in its bones.

1353 Grant Avenue, 397-3751

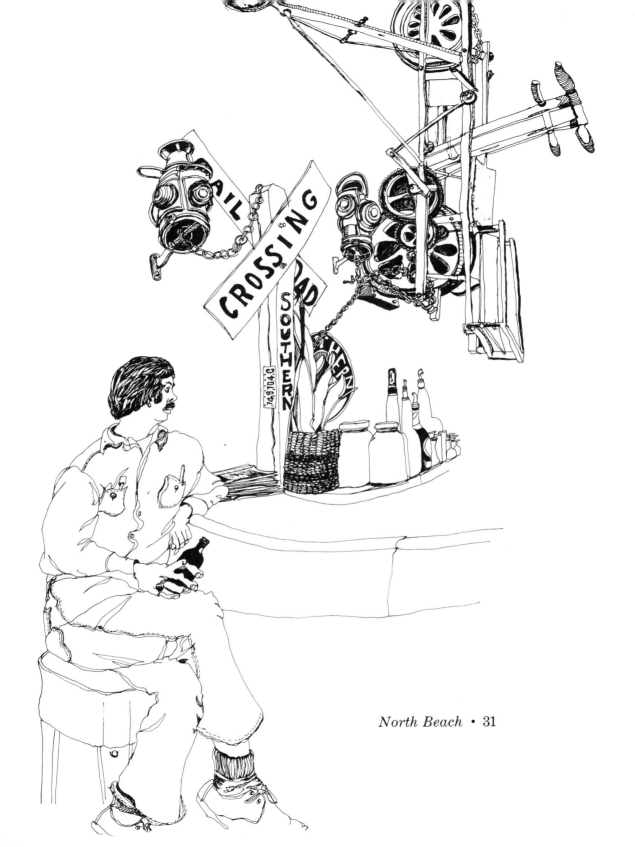

Savoy Tivoli

S HADES OF NORTH AFRICA, more or less; from the outside, with its potted palms, striped awning and Spanish brick and tile exterior, the Savoy Tivoli is a strange looking animal even for Grant Street.

The decor, fanciful as it is, seems to have been the end product of a head-on collision between Moorish and art deco. Painted chickens roost on real molding, with real eggs sitting next to them. The cruise ship in a mural dominating one wall is the same ship in a framed photo on another.

Until 1968, the Savoy Tivoli had been the New Tivoli. With the new name came a brand new look. The present owner is a great auction goer, and his acquisitions are evident throughout.

The cabaret and nightclub entertainment reflect as much creativity as the design. At the height (or depth, according to viewpoint) of the disco craze, the Savoy offered a continental serving of rock, reggae, New Wave and other forms of music. The San Francisco play "Beach Blanket Babylon" metamorphosed from improvisational acting in one of its several back rooms. And local jazz luminaries, Eddie Henderson and Bishop Norman Williams among them, have played here.

The Savoy Tivoli defies a categorical description. In its colorful, if slightly schizophrenic cluster of rooms, someone such as Allen Ginsberg is likely to be found sitting next to a financial district three-piece suiter sipping champagne while a punk rocker strolls by. The balance struck between mildly dissolute and vaguely enchanting survives admirably.

1438 Grant Avenue, 362-7024

Gino & Carlo

COLUMNIST WARREN HINCKLE once wrote an elegy of sorts for a man he called "Gino and Carlo's senior citizen... the patron saint of alcoholics on Green Street." It still hangs on a wall there.

Giovanni Pignatelli clearly had not been a gentleman of delicate disposition or drinking habits, two traits which suited him admirably for G and C. When asked if Giovanni might, through great effort of course, be brought around to respectability, poet Bob Kauffman retorted, "Why turn a perfectly good frog into a prince?"

Why indeed. Gino and Carlo is a perfectly good frog of a saloon, called at times "the most famous unknown bar in the world." The regulars, which is to say the entire brood, are a cross section of North Beach locals and quasi-locals, all very protective of their haunt. Due largely to its anonymously tacky exterior and matching interior, G and C is bereft of tourists, who pass it by for more obvious havens of distinction. Which is fine, because you come by not for the casual quaff. You come by to drink.

Its low profile notwithstanding, G and C has long been a drinking landmark in the city. On a busy night, the saloon has all the order and decorum of a beach invasion under heavy fire, Italian chasing English all about the room and heated debates in progress on everything from Marcuse's philosophy to the relative merits of halter tops on large-breasted women. The common denominator, though, is sports.

A raft of trophies bear moot testimony to the prowess of the saloon's teams. But pool trophies predominate, that sport being the consuming passion of the bar. Its teams tend to dominate the city finals, and its own tournament is taken with appropriate gravity. Photos of winners and losers are everywhere on the walls.

A near total lack of windows and an atmosphere best described as Early Ralph Kramden lends G and C that cherished dark and smoky dinginess guaranteed to drive off all but the most dedicated of drinkers. Slightly bedraggled and belligerent, unhampered by respectability and of devoutly Italian ancestry, Gino and Carlo commands a loyalty of its regulars unmatched by any other bar.

548 Green Street, 421-0896

36 • *North Beach*

New Pisa

ONE GENRE OF GREAT SALOON, and perhaps the finest, sets well apart from the rest. These noble establishments have images irretrievably mingled with those of their owners, to the inestimable good of both.

Witness the New Pisa and Dante Benedetti. Where one begins and the other leaves off is not always so easy to tell. The secret of the former is the vast warmth of the latter, a man with the stocky frame and rolling gait of an ex-boxer and inveterate coach, and a welling paisano's grin big enough to fill the whole place. He rolled his two grand passions, sports and cookery, into one fine restaurant.

The New Pisa is an unrelentingly decent place in a sometimes manic neighborhood, with a proper blend of old world and old school spirits. His vast collection of sports esoterica, from antique football programs to autographed photos of athletes and the like, compete with assorted items of history, such as an autographed photo of the Iwo Jima flag raising. Innumerable college pennants ring the room like a surrey fringe, but the centerpiece is an oil painting of Dan Benedetti, dressed in the uniform he once wore as coach of the University of San Francisco baseball team.

Even if the mustard-colored walls are plastered with Dan's great sporting lore, the regulars stay loyal for a better reason than that. To call the New Pisa a sports bar is only a start; like calling Dan Benedetti a sportsman. Both are a good deal more, built from good times and hard knocks together, and the city is richer for both.

550 Green Street, 362-4726

Washington Square Bar & Grill

WHEN WRITER HERB GOLD wrote "It's Out to talk about an In restaurant," he had his current favorite haunt, the Washington Square Bar and Grill, firmly in mind. That admonition aside, he went on to laud its virtues nonetheless.

In fact, other writers have lauded the WSB&G's virtues as well, it appearing not infrequently in the press, and almost invariably with a prodigious list of famous patrons included. Politicians, literati, North Beach boheme and what-have-you rub shoulders. Undoubtedly its inner circle of devotees boasts one of the highest quotients of wit, intelligence and humor of any bar in the city.

Who can argue with a place that publishes its own newspaper, albeit on a highly irregular basis? Or whose softball team would suffer nothing less than playing another team in Paris for its first away game ever? (Its second, an artful victory in England, left their record unblemished on the road.) One has to forgive a slight air of arrogance under the circumstances.

The WSB&G is two rooms, well lit and with a slightly too significant decibel level that comes from its being crowded much of the time. The off-hours are better for alcoholic meditation. Owners Ed Moose and Sam Deitsch preside, the former with a diplomatic bent and the latter with a sharpened, sometimes caustic wit. As Sam readily points out, an Irish-Jewish duo operating an Italian restaurant in a Chinese neighborhood, was bound for greatness from the start.

The motif is Third Avenue, New York, to the extent any exists, with the thread of a cable car theme running throughout to localize it. Stylish but largely unadorned, the WSB&G peers out on Washington Square and St. Peter and Paul Cathedral across the street.

Political and business deals are born here commonly. The establishment has seen marriages, wakes and even a funeral on its premises. The piano is taken over every night, with the occasional appearance of a great, such as Earl "Fatha" Hines

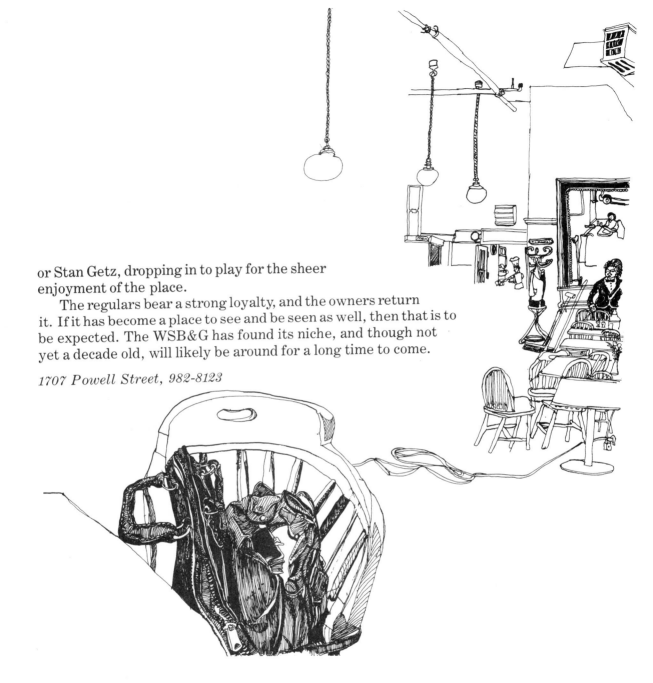

or Stan Getz, dropping in to play for the sheer
enjoyment of the place.

   The regulars bear a strong loyalty, and the owners return
it. If it has become a place to see and be seen as well, then that is to
be expected. The WSB&G has found its niche, and though not
yet a decade old, will likely be around for a long time to come.

1707 Powell Street, 982-8123

Cookie's Star Buffet

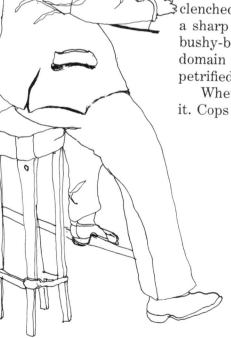

THEY BELLOW "COOKIE," or "Cook," or, strangest to the ear, "Lawrence." They love him, call him a celebrity. Him, Lawrence "Cookie" Picetti, master of all you survey at 708 Kearney and barkeep emeritus, a celebrity; he shrugs it off.

He isn't, after all, what could be called inaccessible, having presided at his bar five days a week nearly non-stop for four decades. Nor is Cookie's Star Bar a paragon of style exactly. Aside from hundreds of autographed photos of faces famous and familiar that have paid their respects at Cookie's roadside shrine (Jerry Brown's "all the best" languishes behind the jukebox), the decor is unremarkable. But the walls are loaded with decades of San Francisco faces and places, an insider's history of the city second to none.

Since the doors opened back in 1942, the bar appears to have changed as little as Cookie. The former has settled into comfortable inactivity, ignoring the shifting tides of public whim. If ever the crusty, worn-out look leaps to the forefront of popular taste, Cookie's will be the rage.

He has a hawkbill nose, an omnipresent Santa Fe cigar clenched between his teeth and a deadpan delivery that cloaks a sharp wit. Constancy has been collecting with age on the bushy-browed scion of San Francisco saloons and his humble domain like a liberal layer of dust. Both have a pleasantly petrified air about them.

When the old Hall of Justice was nearby, Cookie's catered to it. Cops and crooks, judges, lawyers and city politicos rubbed elbows at the bar. The chemistry of the crowd has been altered somewhat.

Keep an eye out for the battered blue-glass entry and the neon sign over the door, as missing it is easy. Cookie should be there, he's not planning on going anywhere. "I was born on this street and I'll die on this street," he has declared. And not for a long time, God willing.

708 Kearney Street, 362-5167

Red's Place

FROM THE OUTSIDE looking in, the bar hunkers in smoky darkness. You discern some cracked old pagoda-roofed mirrors, a couple of aged pinball machines and an incessantly humming fan, all lit by an overhead fluorescent tube, the lone survivor in a cluster of dead sockets.

Red's Place has been holed up on Jackson Street since 1937, a grizzly, recalcitrant Chinatown fixture happily free of any redeeming social value.

Red was an American and a patriot, a veteran of World War I. His picture still hangs on the back bar. His son Junior, now grown old himself, is the bar's proprietor, spending much of his day parked at the end of the bar nearest the door playing cards with a few of his older regulars from Chinatown.

Beyond a couple of decrepit linoleum tables and wooden chairs, furnishings are sparse. And from the look of the joint, the extent of maintenance since the doors opened has been the very occasional removal of the empty beer bottles stacked against the wall. If Junior wanted to make more money, he'd buy good pourspouts to measure his drinks, or fix the bar, or something. But he doesn't. The finest cognac is $1.35.

As the sign on the old register says: "I have no drinking problem; I drink, I get drunk, I fall down. No problem."

Joking, and like Red's Place, a little defiant.

No problem.

672 Jackson Street, 362-9676

Paoli's

ERHAPS THE BEST THING about Paoli's is gone now, banished by the Health Department. Among all of Joe Paoli's memorabilia, his eclectic collection of flags and photos, of antiques, sports trinkets and military service articles and the like, this one stood out. Literally. A huge stuffed Kodiac bear turned more than one diner's eye, more than one celebrant's head when it came rolling down Montgomery on wheels in a St. Patrick's Day parade. Being the progressive bunch they were, however, the Health Department ruled that hairy animals and restaurants didn't mix, so it had to go.

Plenty of other items remain. Joe Paoli used to be a pretty good boxer, so some of the photos are of old boxers, like Kid Chocolate and Bobo Wilson. Joe was a Navy machine-gunner in World War II, so the services are well represented on the walls of his establishment. A flag from the San Quentin chapter of the American Legion here, a water pump bolted to the bar there; in the subdued yellow light, the artifacts meld well with the dark wood. The saloon has a comfortable, old time, almost smoky aura somewhat different from the standard financial district fare.

In early evening, Paoli's has long been known as a good place to go alone, but not be alone, largely because of the popularity of some of the best free hors d'oeuvres in town. Darryl Hutchins on piano most nights is nearly as much a fixture as anything in the saloon, and musicians drop by unannounced to play along.

Since 1951, Paoli's has been going strong, though not always at its present spot. It has carved its own niche downtown, a niche all manner of people fill.

565 Commercial Street, 781-7115

Harrington's

WHEN THEY GOT OFF THE BOAT at last, they got off young, strong and hungry for work, but poor and green as all Ireland to the ways of a new world. And often the first place they came was Harrington's on Front Street.

For a barkeep was a good deal more then. He was a paragon in Irish society playing arbiter, welfare agency, banker and philosopher by turn. Leo Harrington could always help. He found them jobs off the boat, a place to stay, even loaned them money. They gathered at his bar and by and large minded themselves. Far better to be 86'd from church back then than from Harrington's. The crowd may have been rough, but he commanded its respect.

When Leo Harrington finally died in 1959, it seemed half the city of San Francisco turned out. Ten motorcycle cops escorted a procession a mile long; he had been that kind of man.

Little hints at Ireland in this San Francisco landmark now. Aside from a few wall-size prints of ships, and the addition of a newer, slightly fancier second bar and fireplace, the style is basically utilitarian. No backbar from around the Horn, the acoustic ceiling shows water stains and the skylights are purely functional. Henry Harrington, Leo's father, opened several saloons in the city, this being the only one left still run by the Harrington clan. But it still can and does draw hellacious crowds.

One of the brothers who runs the place, Robert, has a myriad of tales to tell of the old days, working as a boy here. Like opening the doors at six a.m. and bam! The men packing the bar, downing three quick shots and a beer then back to work at the printer's shops or produce jobs nearby; the blue collar coffee break. The iceman who once casually flipped a 50-pound block of ice up onto his little finger, balancing it while he slowly finished his drink. Or the man who grabbed him fiercely once, all of his toes and fingers broken, telling him to be tough was nothing; get an education.

It was a drinking man's saloon, nothing romantic about it;

just the focal point of a lot of lives led in quiet, accepting desperation. Life is a good deal different now, and better. With the expansion of the financial district and the building of the Embarcadero Center, the blue collars turned white, but business is steady as ever.

Robert still hears echoes of O'Neill here, of "The Iceman Cometh" and that whole social milieu that has vanished now. "We've gone from a saloon to a pub," he says, only to add wryly, "but we're not yet a cocktail lounge."

245 Front Street, 392-7595

Schroeder's

HANGING AMONG THE PLETHORA of memorabilia on the restaurant's paneled walls is an official document from the late Mayor Moscone. "WHEREAS," the proclamation intones, "Mr. Kniesche and his family have owned and operated Schroeder's Cafe since 1921 and WHEREAS Schroeder's has been a proud San Francisco institution since 1893 the city of San Francisco honors T. Max Kniesche on his 90th birthday."

Tradition. It flows as thick as good German beer throughout, enhanced by the white-aproned waiters, their meticulous service, and by Herman Richter's life-size murals of German life painted in 1933, by the cane chairs and polished oak tables and the massive mahogany rosewood bar, by every element that makes up this old world hof-brau. The very air is redolent of that slightly formal, masculine dignity so familiar to the financial district.

Henry Schroeder, a burly German immigrant, opened his restaurant on Market Street in 1893. A victim of the earthquake and fire, Schroeder's was reincarnated temporarily where the armory stands now, at 16th and Mission. Housed in several different locations on Front Street, it finally came to rest on its present spot in 1956.

From the day the doors opened, it was a male bastion for merchants, sea captains and businessmen. Its chauvinism was tempered, if only slightly, in 1935, when women were allowed to dine here. After 1:30 p.m., of course. Not until 1970 was the custom withdrawn.

Three generations of Kniesches have managed and worked at Schroeder's. A virtual shrine to Max Sr., who bought the restaurant from Henry Schroeder, occupies the front, along with another to Schroeder. The walls are filled with testimonials to the establishment. Tradition is honored. Without it, with any substantial change, it would be something other than Schroeder's. And not as good.

240 Front Street, 421-4778

Templebar

F RUMOR BE TRUE, the Templebar once housed one of the city's most luxurious brothels. If not, it certainly should have. The crystal chandeliers, dimly lit, the red-velvet aura, the gilt-framed mirrors, the wood shutters, and of course the plush staircase beckoning to a more secluded upstairs do little to dissuade the skeptic.

Nor will the Templebar ever be faulted for high visibility, secreted at the end of tiny Tillman Place as it is. The two buildings to its fore seem to have been slammed up against the front, sparing room for a door and little more.

Housed in the first structure rebuilt after the earthquake, it has a venerable history. The Templebar functioned in comfortable obscurity until "Davey" Davenport bought it for three hundred dollars on the eve of Prohibition and began to serve a highly popular, if slightly suspect, libation in its silver teapots.

The backbar may be the finest in all the city, a massive, brooding piece with flowing arches, finely carved from rosewood and birch. Fashioned in 1849 after the famous Temple Bar of London, it had the good fortune to be stored in the charmed Hotaling Warehouse when the quake and fire hit, avoiding a grievous fate.

Sketches of the original Temple Bar and renderings of an infant San Francisco add to the discreet, aristocratic humor that prevails. It must have been a beautiful brothel, but failing that, it makes a superlative saloon.

1 Tillman Place, 362-6661

Hoffman's Grill

POP SULLIVAN PATTERNED HIS establishment after one in 1880s New York, or so the story goes. He brought Hoffman's into the world at 2nd and Market, only to see it depart again abruptly in 1906 when it was reduced to an ignominious pile of rubble by the quake. Pop escaped with his life and his oil paintings, and, undaunted, reopened his restaurant the next year at its present site.

Little has changed in this German hofbrau. Its masculine tenor has yielded grudgingly, if at all, to the advances of time. Women were banished to an eyrie overlooking the main floor until little more than a decade ago. Men, after all, were rolling dice at the bar, and a female's presence was inhibiting, to say the least.

Even the smell is that comforting mixture of antiseptic and spice peculiar to older, well-heeled saloons. The old brass chandeliers are reassuringly dusty, the oil paintings suitably old and their gilt frames ornate. The crowd remains a hearty one, their laughter echoing off the tile floor to the polished mahogany beams overhead.

The lord of the saloon is none other than the redoubtable Sean Mooney, an Irish guru of sorts freely dispensing good will, opinions and blarney in equal amounts.

Until recently, progress in the form of a highrise threatened to close the battered wood and brass doors of Hoffman's, but designation as a historical landmark brought a reprieve. That is the best of news, because the financial district can ill afford to lose the last vestiges of its better days.

619 Market Street, 421-1467

House of Shields

"Enter these portals and forget time and care."
(Sign posted at the House of Shields, gone now.)

EVERYTHING CHANGES, even the House of Shields. Eddie Shields would have groused no end about that, but there you are anyway. No clocks in his saloon, he said adamantly. If you don't have the time you don't belong here in the first place. No televisions, either; "I'm running a saloon, not a theater" was his retort.

What he was running, what the House of Shields has always been, is a men's drinking club. Women weren't even allowed in until 1972. It has been a place of business in more ways than one, countless deals having been sealed and broken here over the past decades. So many men in three-piece suits have come and gone that in places their heels have worn through the floor to the original mosaic tile below.

The bartenders are amiable, genteel masters of the art. Animal heads and bronze statues of semi-clad nymphs line the oak and mahogany walls. Brass spittoons are spaced evenly along the only stand-up bar in the city. Even the light is cold, which is just fine, thank you. Not a plant, not a piece of stained glass softens the old New York mood. A fern would die of sheer intimidation in this place.

The House of Shields sold a while back. The layers of nicotine that over the years blackened the walls are gone, the wood restored. Major restoration is in the wind to vanquish the worn down look that has accumulated, and to re-create what began with Eddie Shields. All part of the change, whether the old timers at the House of Shields think much of it or not. After all, nothing stays the same.

39 New Montgomery Street, 392-7732

Happy Valley Bar

FACT AND LEGEND about the Palace Hotel, the grande dame of San Francisco hostelries, are hopelessly mixed. Its bars seem particularly prone to this.

No one speaks with absolute certainty on the ancestry of the Happy Valley. But everything its more renowned neighbor the Pied Piper is not, the Happy Valley has been. Large, bright and sometimes, boisterous, the Pied Piper is dominated by a massive Maxfield Parrish painting for which the bar was named. Well-heeled men have historically met for business, pleasure and drink there, but until 1964, women were barred entrance.

Hence the Happy Valley; women gathered in the Pied Piper's smaller, darker, and definitely more mysterious companion. And thus the Happy Valley quite naturally gathered the Pied Piper's attention.

At some point, it may have housed a men's haberdashery. Now the polished redwood panel walls are adorned with pre-earthquake bric-a-brac and artifacts dating from the first opening of the Palace Hotel in 1875. Leaded-glass chandeliers, red-velvet curtains, discreet lighting and an intimate mood contrast with the immenseness of the rest of the hotel. Behind the bar hangs a rendering of Happy Valley, the city's first settlement.

Time seems to have slowed almost to a stillness here, where the elegance of old San Francisco is lovingly preserved. From its grand inception, the Palace served as social arbiter in the city, a magnificent draw to wealth and power. A glint of this survives in the Happy Valley, undimmed.

Sheraton-Palace Hotel, Market and New Montgomery
392-8600

Redwood Room

ET'S LIFT A GLASS to the old days, to the Redwood Room of yore. To its days in the eye of the high society storm, to the 1950s, when its newsletter "Day and Night" was published once, sometimes twice a month; everybody who was anybody appeared in its pages. When dignitaries came to San Francisco, they came often as not to the Redwood Room. In an era when women were not seen alone in bars, women went unescorted to the Redwood Room without fear of being bothered.

Judy Garland is rumored to have had a regular table here, but then this perennial favorite of the after-theater crowd has fostered all sorts of delicious rumors. Why else would the old photos show that a young Herb Caen made it a stop of his?

It can still be the sort of place that leaves a person feeling naked without a tie; where the act of holding a wine glass can be elevated to an art, and the tinkling of china and crystal from the nearby buffet seems an immensely appropriate sound.

Actually, the Redwood Room grows a good deal louder than that much of the time. Since being built in 1933, designed by the same man who created the Opera House interior, the Clift Hotel's palatial paneled bar has been a traditional high-society hang-out. No barstools are to be found, only upholstered chairs, marble tables and ornate bar chairs.

Over the years, the beautiful twenty-foot panels of burnished redwood darkened, languishing under annual coats of varnish that were applied out of some misguided sense of preservation. Then, in a massive 1976 restoration, the walls and pillars were stripped and refinished. To everyone's surprise, a mural of inlaid wood reappeared over the bar. The immense art-deco lamps, each looking like a stack of teacups with progressively larger saucers, were preserved. For a room entirely of redwood, the saloon is surprisingly and pleasantly bright.

The close-knit high society that fed the mystique of the Redwood Room has faded somewhat, and so inevitably has the

mystique. But a toast to its aristocratic style nonetheless, for what remains is an architectural work of art.

Geary and Taylor Streets, 775-4700

Top of the Mark

"THE HILL OF PALACES" Robert Louis Stevenson once called Nob Hill, a name both lyrical and accurate. Crocker, Stanford and Huntington virtually ruled California from their mansions here.

Nearly twenty years after the Mark Hopkins Institute of Art, originally Mark Hopkins's opulent home, burned in the 1906 fire, the Hotel Mark Hopkins rose on the site. It drew San Francisco's high society like a magnet, fast becoming the elegant pinnacle in a city enamored of elegance: Number One Nob Hill.

The peak of the pinnacle came in 1939 with the opening of the Top of the Mark. It offered an unequaled view of the city then, spreading out in an uninterrupted circle below. In World War II, one corner, "The Weeping Corner," became infamous as the final meeting place for men going to war and the women they were leaving behind.

Over time, the skyscrapers have crept upward, tearing into the view. The Bank of America building dwarfs the Top of the Mark now, its Carnelian Room claiming a better vantage point. But the view here is still the sentimental favorite, and the bar retains that air of serenity and assuredness that comes from wealth and being above it all.

Remodeling has given it a modern look, courtesy of mirrored glass, pin-lights in the ceiling and the like. But despite the disco overtones, the Top of the Mark still makes a marvelous perch to watch the world below.

Mark Hopkins Hotel, Number One Nob Hill, 392-3434

Kimball's

HEY CALLED IT THE "HAM AND EGGS FIRE." In a desperate attempt to halt the fire consuming the city in 1906, the Army Corps of Engineers blew up Van Ness Avenue.

The effort failed, however. The Hayes Valley district in general, and the building on the plot where Kimball's now stands, burned to the ground.

The lot served no better use than a parking area until 1922, when a new, all-brick building designed by a well-known architect of the day went up there.

That same building Kimball Allen and his wife took on in 1980 when they set about to open the restaurant. They transformed what was essentially a decomposing brick garage of advanced years into an earthquake proof, blessed-by-the-planning-commission establishment that fairly reeks of gentility.

To be fair, that gentility comes more from the clientele than the structure itself. Kimball's strategic positioning across from the symphony hall made the tenor of its clientele a foregone conclusion from the beginning. Opera and symphony buffs and performers themselves adopted Kimball's as their pre- and post-performance retreat.

The decor is thoroughly modern, with art gallery overtones. An open mezzanine girdles the restaurant, peering down on a piano played every evening. Jazz and classical music drift unobtrusively out of the walls.

If the fledgling Kimball's represents anything, it is the broader Hayes Valley renaissance, with its suitable reverence towards the old architecture. The only drawback to Kimball's is its greatest asset: its close alliance with the performing arts. Only time will tell if more than that crowd will take to it.

300 Grove Street, 861-5555

Buena Vista

SOMEWHERE BETWEEN DEATH AND TAXES is a far more palatable certainty: Irish coffee at the Buena Vista. The "BeeVee" has been tucked away a block up from the base of Hyde Street since the 1890s, coming into its own one night in 1952 when Chronicle columnist Stanton Delaplane, fresh back from Ireland, introduced this saloon to the Irish coffee.

Since then, barkeeps here have served a numbing number of the concoctions, in excess of 10 million at last cont. An Irish at the BeeVee is as much a tradition as anything in the city.

On a clear day, the bar is a fine roost from which to watch the eternal Beach Street promenade and the bay beyond. By night the view is good, providing one can find a table, an accomplishment roughly akin to staking a claim at the height of a gold rush.

At such times the 16 bar stools are at least 200 too few, the whole place looking like some overstuffed Pullman car forever stalled on the tracks, its charges happily drinking away shoulder to shoulder.

Brightly lit, with doors at both ends, picture windows, a counter dispensing food as well as drink, and a total absnce of romantic corners and alcoves, the BeeVee definitely cannot be counted on for privacy. The decor is a half-hearted attempt at best, with crested beer plaques, framed articles, old photos and various renderings of the premises all that is happening in the way of ambience.

Still, the Buena Vista remains a traditional meeting place for many locals and tourists alike. When the tourist trade rose in numbers, the regulars decreased proportionately, abandoning their beloved BeeVee for less-frequented pastures. Some remain, however, and the cosmopolitan crowd provides a rare warmth.

2765 Hyde Street, 474-5044

Eagle Cafe

FOR HALF A CENTURY the Eagle Cafe clung to the waterfront virtually unchanged. It was home-away-from-home, often the only home, for a rugged crew of seamen and longshoremen, sea captains and even writers.

It was the rallying point for the violent longshoremen's strike in 1933, and a final breakfast stop for an unlucky few before the short trip to Alcatraz. All in all, the Eagle has never been a well-bred sort of place, but it's always been an honest one.

Then, in 1978, the wheels of progress brought Pier 39. The Eagle would have to go, but it didn't go far. The building was hoisted lock, stock and beerbarrel to a perch on the new pier. Nothing changed but the view, with all the years of memorabilia, the eulogies and photos and cryptic messages whose meanings an outsider can only guess at still lining the walls.

And it has more than held its own in a sea of knick-knack shops, a fragment of an older city now largely gone by the boards. In the new-made-to-look-old slickness of Pier 39, the Eagle still dishes out some of the cheapest meals and booze around. The tables are linoleum, the bay view great, and the atmosphere pure clipper ship.

The Eagle itself hasn't changed, but the crowd has. The old-timers are largely gone, victims of containerized shipping, parking problems, and most of all time. T.H. Watkins, a writer and Eagle patron, wrote the best eulogy when it was uprooted, signalling an end to an era that was dying anyway. "To Jeannie and Johnny and Baptiste and Hohn and Cheyenne and Roger and Wild Bill and Cuz and Mike and Eddie and Gabi and Charles and those whose memories are ghosts at the bottom of every glass.

"How do you say goodbye?

"You don't.

"You remember."

Pier 39, 433-3689

Pier 23

PEOPLE FORGET. They forget the waterfront is a world away from the financial district, and should have stayed there. But they do things like Pier 39 and the whole Wharf madness to it, sometimes in good faith and sometimes not. They argue good arguments, but they are economic wolves in philosophic sheep's clothing. The bottom line is almost always bucks.

And yes, maybe the waterfront is dead, shipping brought to a slow, choking end by change, leaving the few seamen and longshoremen who stuck it out to ponder what happened.

A few barnacled crusty slices of the old days still remain, where the paint still gets to peel off on its own and nothing has been fancied up really. What makes them better is your gut says they're honest.

Sitting and staring through the backbar windows at the Pier 23 Cafe, out across the bay at Oakland, you thank God they haven't thought up a way to float gift shops on water yet. Daytime here means a good lunchtime crowd and a chance to check out what's on the walls: Burt Reynolds au naturale, some fishnet slung from the ceiling, other photos; but mostly just a good ramshackle interior in general.

Nighttime pulls the joint into fast-lane Dixieland, courtesy of Jack "Jive" Shafer and the Rhythm Rascals. A miracle then is a table to keep for the evening; good luck a place to stand. Jack blows a mean horn, and supposedly blew it with Louis Armstrong. Grinning and squinting like he does, he looks a bit like his old partner.

Anyway, the whole place shakes and rattles enough to break moorings. No cover and no bouncer since Whitey the owner decided they were both more or less immoral.

The building's nearly sixty years old. Boats used to dock here and pass their crab catch through the back window for sale. Music's a tradition. Before Whitey took over twenty or more years ago, tales tell of a mountainous black man named Abigail ("Abbey" for short), who would come in between stints as a merchant marine. He sang in an off-key alto accompanied by piano, and usually brought the house down.

Scenes from several movies have been shot here, as well as a t.v. pilot and several episodes from, of course, *The Streets of San Francisco*. The reality-hungry scouts come looking and find what they want; what a waterfront used to be.

Musicians wander in late all the time after their own acts somewhere else, to jam or just listen. Tallulah Bankhead would occasionally bring an entourage down to pay their respects.

Sit here long enough and the sense comes that if Whitey ever felt the need to change anything, he'd be smart enough to forget it. Sell out for a few bucks? It'll never pay in the long run.

Pier 23, 362-5125

Bouncer's

WHEN THE FLEET IS IN, don't ever try to hide from it at Bouncer's. Crews blow in here en masse, elbow to elbow with the usual core of waterfront life, laughing and shouting and getting the better of a bottle until it gets the better of them. Tourist and chic has yet to make it as far as this neighborhood.

Once San Francisco started getting more civilized and pretty, she had the good sense not to ask Bouncer's along for the ride. The exterior walls of peeling plaster look as rough and honest as the crowd inside. The old tile floor has been worn through in spots, and varnish on the bar carried away on countless elbows. A long time ago, the water splashed almost on the doorstep, but with docks and piers and progress no one shoves off from the door any longer.

A lot of flotsam and jetsam has been beached at Bouncer's over the years, giving the place its cluttered character. An arsenal of whaling harpoons dangles overhead, and the walls are filled with old photos, mugs, street signs, pennants, trophies, posters and bits and pieces of personal lives left behind by patrons who felt like adding a fragment of themselves to the place. Its collection of Coral Sea crewmen's hats is second to none.

People whose lives are tied to the waterfront invariably know Bouncer's. A lot of its regulars see it as just a little more than a crusty whiskey bar and cafe. They see it like home.

64 Townsend Street, 397-2480

Mission Rock Resort

WEEKENDS ARE THE FINEST times. Everyone drifts down to roost for awhile. On warm, slow and sunny afternoons, they join each other on the poopdeck to drink beer and shoot the bull, wearing the Mission Rock Resort like some old, comfortable shirt that fits right.

"Resort" may not be the most accurate label in the world to pin on it. It has burned and been rebuilt several times, having clung to the China Basin waterfront in one form or another for more than thirty years. It hadn't amounted to much by the time Bob and Norma Wahl bought the place several years ago. What they inherited was a one-room beer, bait and burger joint, a few boats they promptly dubbed the "Leaky Tikis" and a small but

devoted bunch of regulars.

Before long, the Mission Rock had grown appendages: upstairs with a dining room, downstairs with a dance floor and outward with a broad expanse of deck for keeping track of the shipyards and freighters. A hi-fi dispenses tunes through one of those old, steel speakers that looks like an inverted brake drum nailed to the wall. Everything sounds like Eddie Cantor on 78, but it's good enough. Making the deckrails as wide as they did was a fit of architectural genius.

Nothing exotic but everything right draws all manner of people, and more all the time. Short of burning again, and Bob and Norma giving up, it should be around unchanged for a long time to come.

817 China Basin, 621-5538

Twin Peaks Tavern

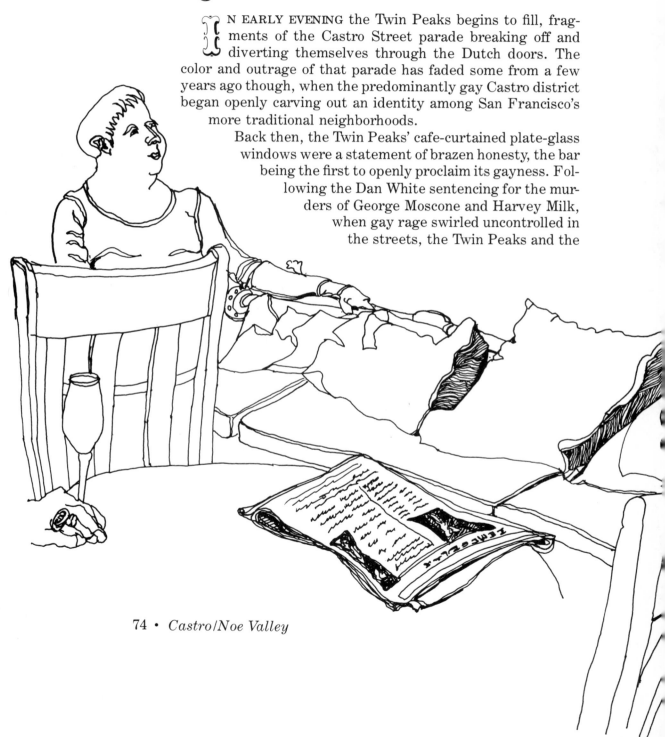

IN EARLY EVENING the Twin Peaks begins to fill, fragments of the Castro Street parade breaking off and diverting themselves through the Dutch doors. The color and outrage of that parade has faded some from a few years ago though, when the predominantly gay Castro district began openly carving out an identity among San Francisco's more traditional neighborhoods.

Back then, the Twin Peaks' cafe-curtained plate-glass windows were a statement of brazen honesty, the bar being the first to openly proclaim its gayness. Following the Dan White sentencing for the murders of George Moscone and Harvey Milk, when gay rage swirled uncontrolled in the streets, the Twin Peaks and the

Elephant Walk found themselves at the center of action.

Sitting at the nexus of Market and Castro streets, it stares out like someone's living room at the street cars and buses rumbling by. The patrons are mostly gay men, a mixture of working and retired folk drawn by the bar's congeniality. The brass and paintings, the sculptured carpet and antiques all disguise what once was a run-down hovel of a bakery. The centerpiece is the ornate backbar, often dressed in flowers, which is one of the few to rightfully claim to have come around the Horn in the 1880s.

With its old prints and gilt mirrors, the Twin Peaks seems as much a salon as a saloon. And if the crowd is slightly less flamboyant and more tempered now than it once was, it is no less amicable.

401 Castro Street, 864-9470

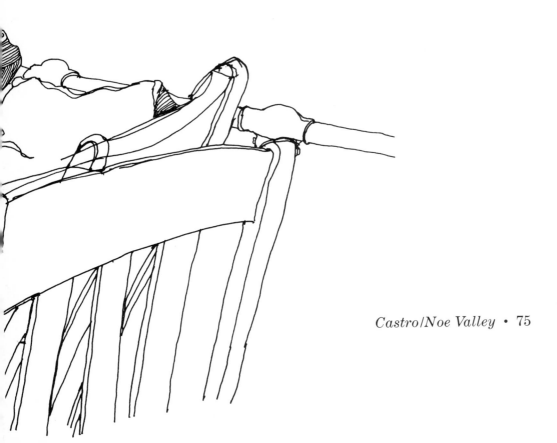

Finnegan's Wake

A T ITS BEST, SAN FRANCISCO the city, becomes an amalgam of neighborhoods, sewn together on the topography like patches on a rumpled quilt. Compared to the frenetic Castro District just over the hill, Noe Valley verges on the bucolic; urban bucolic, mind you, but still a far cry from its neighbor.

When Finnegan's Wake came into the world, it came in Irish, modeled loosely after a Cambridge bar called the Plough and Stars. But what Noe Valley locals wanted was more their own gathering spot, and not Ireland. So Finnegan's Wake lost its brogue.

The jukebox allows for some radical differences of opinion, offering a smorgasbord of punk, country, rock and jazz. Pinball and pool give it the Good Neighborhood Bar seal of approval. And it has its decorative idiosyncracies: works by local artists, the largest collection of ceramic Elvis Presleys anywhere in Noe Valley, and of course the photograph with the inscription "Che—a most uncommon cat. 4 August 69–22 June 79." (Actually, Che appears quite common, but one hesitates to tell that to a bar owner who has Che's furry little visage tatooed on his arm.)

The windows are large, the place light and airy, the crowd lively and young. The owners have allied themselves with their patrons to everyone's advantage, until Finnegan's Wake is home for an extended Noe Valley family.

And given a pint or two, one is even tempted to give Che the benefit of the doubt.

4054 24th Street, 826-9816

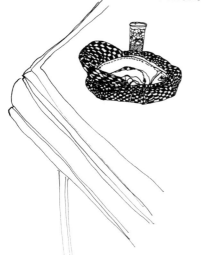

77

Lost Weekend

WELCOME TO THE LOST WEEKEND. Come in, come in. That's Rodney on the organ, up there behind the bar. Been here years and years. The place opened in 1948... nothing but sand dunes in every direction back then. The crowds really started after the Twin Peaks Tunnel was built, and people could take the old Taraval line out here. Remember those old street cars? They were simply great.

The name? Comes from an old Ray Milland movie. You remember it. He played an alcoholic reporter. We get movie buffs in here all the time, and some have seen every movie on the wall posters.

Those are theater curtains in the entry there. The old organ... this one's nice enough, of course... but the old one was a real beauty, a Wurlitzer pipe organ out of the Fox Theater in Oakland. We had to take it out a few years ago, though. Why is a sad story we don't talk about.

No, the decoration hasn't changed much. The leaning glass brick front window, the yellow linoleum bartop, the acoustic ceiling with sparkles; it's all art deco, but it's got a real dignity of its own. So do the people.

We all love it here. We've got folk who've been coming in religiously since it opened. They come in on particular nights of the week, dressed to the nines occasionally (they've got a lot of pride, you know) and sit and drink. They sing along with the organ, maybe clap. The sign says "No Dancing" but sometimes people can't read, if you know what I mean. They've all got respect for the place.

I could tell you stories. Like the politician's wife—you'd know the name if I told you—who came in here potted one night, dressed in nothing but a fur coat. She stood over there by the classical jukebox (the other one's popular) and bared it all.

Or Gertrude Tracy. Gertie was a character, bless her soul, one of the best. Like a Sophie Tucker. She worked the Barbary Coast as a professional entertainer. She's gone now, but she came in all the time. I've got good memories of this place.

Maybe this place settled into some kind of time warp the minute it opened, back when ladies still wore hats and gloves just to go to the grocery store. Back when manners and style really counted. Seems like all the saloons nowadays try so hard to be different they all end up the same. But they truly broke the mold on this place.

For my money, it's the finest bar in town.

But I'm keeping you. Thanks for coming by.

1940 Taravel Street, 564-2838

Beach Chalet

SAY A PRAYER for the old Beach Chalet and for the city that owned it. Since it was losing too much money, they let it be turned into a "nice" bar and restaurant. And now it'll be clean and bright and expensive.

People will remember the old Beach Chalet, the way the wind whipped in off the open sea and slammed into the front of the building, whistling tunes through cracks in its heavy old doors. Maybe the crowd *was* a bit rough toward the end. Maybe they did go for the pool and beer, the pinball and jukebox more than Lucien Lebaudt's wonderful murals. They were a WPA project painted in the early thirties, full of real San Francisco faces. And maybe they didn't feel one way or another about the intricate mosaics, or the magnolia wood balustrade with figures artfully carved into it by Michael von Meyer. But that was another dimension to the beauty of the place.

The place had camaraderie, so much sometimes nobody could talk over the din of it. And nothing but the Great Highway between it and the bounding main; it was a neighborhood bar with no neighborhood, but a large crew of loyal regulars. It was pretty run down, but it was a people's bar at least, and the art, people's art, coming out of the Depression the way it did.

The place had history, too. It was a military headquarters at some point, and the VFW meeting hall upstairs was constantly being used, being rented out. The old Beach Chalet was a place to congregate.

Sometimes bars are like people, they get old and die. Say a prayer for the old place because it was real.

Great Highway, near Fulton Street, 558-3706

Cliff House

IT WAS CONSIDERABLY MORE ELEGANT and imposing at the turn of the century. Four versions of the Cliff House have stood on the site since the mid-19th century, but Mayor Sutro's topped them all. She went up in 1896, the grande dame of the coastline, a seven-story palace of spires and turrets, of wood and seemingly endless expanses of glass.

All that remains of that building now is pictures. It survived the 1906 quake only to perish from an electrical fire in 1907. The structure was rebuilt, but on a less ambitious scale. At the foot of the cliff, the Sutro Baths, constructed in 1894, survived that fire, only to burn to the ground in 1966.

Phineas T. Barnacle, the Cliff House bar, has its share of art and artifacts. The mirrors of the backbar are acid-etched with the photographs of Ansel Adams, Adams himself having done the work. But whatever is on the walls, all the maritime objects and mementos and old photos of the Cliff House, nothing surpasses the view. Perched on the edge of the cliff, when the fog rolls in and swallows the coast, the whole building seems detached and hovering in mid-air at land's end. Watch the sunset through what they call God's Window and you will appreciate how this was the culmination of a life-long dream by a Greek immigrant who once ran a hot dog stand down the street.

The bar serves both the neighborhood and bus loads of tourists and is often filled to capacity during the evenings. But on a windblown and sunny day, with the sea a turbulent white and blue, a memory of a city long past, of a fragile era of style and grace, still clings to the edges of the Cliff House.

1090 Point Logos Avenue, 386-7630

Maud's

SAN FRANCISCO, CITY OF LOVE. San Francisco, city of tolerance. These were empty words for gays in the 60s. The Alcoholic Beverages Commission wielded its sword of "moral turpitude" and gay bars officially didn't exist. Women were banned from tending bar unless they owned the saloon.

Before Maud's came into being, this Haight District bar was called The Study. It became Maud's Study for a time, the name being a sort of lesbian code for its patrons. Women going to "The Study" were women likely to be going to the library if overheard.

Times have changed a good deal since it opened, Maud's having become a settled and reasonably respectable member of the neighborhood business clan. Likely the oldest single-owner, single-location lesbian bar in the country, its walls are filled with public notices for events and benefits for the women's community, gay and straight, mingling with snapshots of Maud's regulars and their parties. Pool tables and pinball provide entertainment.

Like so many other saloons that succeed, Maud's is more than just a place to drink; it fills a need. It serves as a women's center as well. If men are not always welcome, it's only because they have no valid reason to come.

Many of the women are young here, and many have made a choice. Some may still be finding themselves. But the sense of comfort and safety makes it a haven for alternatives.

937 Cole Street, 731-6119

Jane Chamberlain

The Anxious Asp

ANXIOUS ASP. Born, 1958. Lived on Green Street in North Beach for nearly a decade, serving beer and wine, with dancing and occasional live music when musicians wandered in. Friend of Vesuvio's and Spec's, friend of the Coffee House, a true pillar of North Beach bohemia. It was a small, street brawler sort of bar back then, with a mixed bag of patrons: gays, blacks and artists, as well as people who bore many other labels.

Even the name was a revolt. It was as close as the owners could come to The Anxious Ass and keep the benediction of the alcoholic beverages board. Died 1967 of legal problems, roughly at the same time as the death of North Beach at the hands of tourists.

Resurrected 1976, on Haight Street. It was the same Asp, but it had shed one skin for another. The old North Beach crowd came by for a time, but soon faded away, taking their fights with them. You can't go home again. The new Anxious Asp was cut from the mold of the new rage, the wood-and-fern bar, but the fern part died when nobody wanted to take care of the plants.

Call it black and cool, now, with an older crowd than the former bar. The disco and dancefloor draw most of the attention. Shaft would feel at home.

People change and communities change, and bars change with them. The new Asp is larger and slightly more sedate than the Asp of old, and people still remember the latter. Same snake, the message says here, just a different skin.

1725 Haight Street, 668-6190

Churchill's

FOR SOME SALOON OWNERS, the birthing of establishments is a career in itself. Once it is properly attired and functioning, the challenge fades.

Churchill's came about in such a way. Its founder is a meticulous architect of saloons. The decor is the result of a frantic burst of creative energy, the original intent of which was to meld a fern bar (back when the phrase could be used without a curled lip and a sneer) and a neighborhood bar.

What resulted was a sort of poor man's Henry Africa's with a wealth of congeniality. Churchill's is an eclectic collection of paintings, posters, old photographs, spittoons and old bottles garnered from anywhere and everywhere, all likely with a personal history that has been lost en route.

On many nights the crowd is largely young and single, packing the place to its guards with a hectic and loud friendliness. Students, merchants, working folk and a garden variety of other types from the immediate neighborhood have adopted Churchill's as their own.

It has been around for eight years now, the successor to Bob's Sports Club and then A Taste of Honey housed in the same spot. Its vibrant mixture reflects the surrounding Clement Street neighborhood, an area that has been one of the great melting pots of the city. The Clement District has seen successive waves of Irish, Russians and Chinese find a home in its streets. Perhaps it is in that fact that Churchill's finds its formula for success, because it is a place a person is as likely to meet someone they've never met as easily as someone they know.

455 Clement Street, 752-0580

Holy City Zoo

PEOPLE DIDN'T ALWAYS stand in line to squeeze into the tiny Holy City Zoo. Nor did comics come in droves. "The business of comedy" yokes two words uncomfortable with each other.

The small, struggling clubs are the grass roots of comedy, and the Holy City was just beginning to grow. But now the crowds and comedians come for some of the best stand-up comedy in the city.

Robin Williams launched his career from Holy City Zoo's stage, and still returns frequently. Michael Pritchard, just now hitting his stride, plays here often. Signs of making it are happening; NBC contracts, Norman Lear and Saturday Night Live auditions, the lights at the end of every amateur comedian's tunnel are starting to shine here.

The size of a good-sized attic, the Holy City Zoo can accomodate about seventy-five people. The interior is made up mostly of beat-up wood, with a few medieval-looking wood slab chairs, tables and booths along the wall opposite the stage. The rudimentary bar has a shingled roof with a raggedy Persian rug on the front. Add a few fake Tiffany lamps and hoards of photos of comedians, some autographed, and you have it. But the comedy-in-a-mineshaft atmosphere is intimate, and it clicks.

The name, so the story goes, came with the furnishings, which the original owner collected during a pass through Holy City, California. He got a free sign, "Holy City Zoo," thrown in with the deal, and rather than buy a new one, well . . . Eccentricity and the Holy City Zoo are inescapable partners. Good comedy, after all, demands that.

408 Clement Street, 752-2846

THE PLOUGH and THE STARS
IRISH PUB and Restaurant

124

Plough & the Stars

THEY CALL THE PLOUGH AND STARS an Irish bar, which is true only in part. Irish-American would be closer still, but a workingman's bar for any nationality would be closest of all. The hangings on the walls tout the battle of the working class with messages like "Come Workers Sing A Rebel Song" and "Peace, Work and Class Politics." The theme is clear: the struggle for a free Ireland is a small part of the greater struggle against oppression. The sense of political commitment sets the Plough and Stars apart from the rest of the Irish bars of the city.

Much of Ireland past and present lives on the walls here, in the old photographs and hundred-year-old tracts from Irish newspapers. There are dartboards too of course, and darts for sale, leagues to be joined and tournaments to be entered. Still more of Ireland is celebrated between them though. At night the hard heels of stepdancers hammer out a staccato rhythm to the traditional Irish music of fiddle and music box, while the Guinness flows.

Perhaps a third are Irish, at least when the music plays, dark haired men and women filling the room with their brogue. The name itself is the symbol of the Irish Citizens Army, drawn from the following quote in the first part of this century: "Ireland belongs to the people from the sod to the stars."

As all things Irish, even those in San Francisco, the Plough and Stars bears an edge of sadness from a war thousands of miles away, that pinball or pool tables or darts or Guinness will never dispell. Freedom alone can give that.

116 Clement Street, 751-1122

Liverpool Lil's

SOMETIMES BARS GET BETTER with age, and sometimes with new owners, and sometimes with both. Less than a decade ago this was the "Liontamer," a seedy little dive so without redeeming social value it was off-limits to personnel from the Presidio across the street.

Liverpool Lil's succeeded it, a small neighborhood tavern with a decor that is thoroughly English, provided the observer closes one eye and cheats a bit with the other. The light is comfortably dim, filtering in through the stained glass bay windows at the front, and the walls and ceilings are cluttered with all manner of mementos worthy of Grandmother's attic.

Five minutes is a lifetime to get acquainted here. The locals and staff alike are a loyal family, a sharp-witted and intelligent young crew, spiced up by the brash good will of a few transplanted East Coasters.

It's not a genuine English pub of course; the Mexican sarape hanging in the dining room sees to that. But the warmth is as genuine, the camaraderie as strong as that between the men of the #2 Eighth Armored Car Company, whose photo graces the backbar. It's a very British bunch in that black and white shot, dated 1936–37. They certainly would have enjoyed it here.

2942 Lyon Street, 921-6664

Paul's Saloon

OCCASIONALLY IT WILL HAPPEN that a busload of foreign tourists, Japanese for instance, will spend an evening at Paul's Saloon. There they sit, broadly smiling and happily incongruous, tapping their toes to some good old down-home bluegrass. They've come looking for America, and figure they've found it.

That of course suits Paul just fine. He won't turn away a soul who behaves himself, good times being the modus operandi of his saloon. An emotionally volatile Burl Ives sort, he sports wire-rimmed glasses, overalls, a fearsome beard and no end of barside philosophy.

In 1969 he shunned his job with a bank for greener pastures, so to speak, when he opened what remains the city's only bluegrass bar. Architectural changes come occasionally at Paul's whim, but with its fireplace full of a decade of uncleaned ashes and a ragged-about-the-edges look, Paul's has nothing in common with the urban cowboy syndrome it will survive. An open and friendly attitude has earned Paul's the reputation as a pleasant spot for unaccompanied women who want to stay that way. No dark corners for the sad and lonely-hearted and no fancy brass, just picking and grinning until the cows come home.

3251 Scott Street, 922-2456

The Chestnut Street Grill

PARADOX IS AT THE HEART of a good saloon. Owned in fact by the proprietor, it succeeds because it is owned in spirit by the people who frequent it. If it belongs to the patrons, then the patrons belong to it.

Zot's discovered that when they opened up their doors on Chestnut Street a few years back, only to sell out a short while later, the crowds having stayed away in droves. What followed was the Chestnut Street Bar and Grill, a living lesson in instant tradition. Just ask any sandwich, or would-be sandwich for that matter.

The brainstorm that struck the owners, was to canonize their friends and patrons, to turn them into a living menu. Make it at the Chestnut Street Bar and Grill and you are ordained as a sandwich, your name gracing one of the selections on the menu. On almost any given night, the place is filled with sandwiches now, happily milling about.

The sense of camaraderie inside the wood and ivory-colored walls is strong, an eternal high school class closeness epitomized by the "class photos" on the front wall: yearbook pictures of the Chestnut Street regulars.

The Chestnut area has changed in recent years, the smaller businesses and older people forced out by inflation. For most of its life since the mid-thirties, the All-Brite club was here. The brass railing at the front corner of the bar is worn through by decades of regulars. But the All-Brite faltered and died, like virtually all the neighborhood bars around it. Now the faces have changed and the bar has too, but the regulars remain as loyal as ever.

2231 Chestnut Street, 922-5558

Pierce St. Annex

TO THE UNWARY, The Pierce Street Annex may prove a shock to the senses. Sure, a singles bar; but openly, flauntingly? Signs issue edicts about "the rules of the game"? "Talk—don't touch," they insist. "If you don't get good vibes, move on." Have a good time, they urge... but be an adult.

It had only been a matter of time until, in 1962, the singles bar finally became institutionalized in The Pierce Street Annex. Six bachelors threw parties in their Pierce Street house that were so loud and frequent they became the bane of their neighborhood. Why not turn those parties into a living, they reasoned. Pre-sexual revolution and pre-Haight Ashbury, San Francisco's first self-proclaimed, unabashed "singles" bar opened.

With its two bars, six-foot television screen and tiny dance-floor, the Annex is both a saloon and a Miss Lonelyhearts Club for extroverts. Charcoal drawings in the style of huge, caricatured heads and comic captions honor the regulars. Photos of past group outings remind locals of all the fun had.

While the Annex professes to offer a structured, congenial alternative to frenetic body shops, on a busy night the uninitiated may have trouble making the distinction. But it has sprouted branches in other cities, and they too do well. Let other bars treat the singles crowd with vague discomfort or disdain. The continued success of The Pierce Street Annex proves solitude isn't all that bad.

3138 Fillmore Street, 567-1400

Balboa Cafe

EVERY OLD SALOON has a tale or two to tell from Prohibition, true or not, usually embellished a bit over time. They give the place an air of permanency and respectability that is part of age.

At the Balboa Cafe people talk about the raid here when a federal agent deftly lept behind the bar without a thought to what might be on the other side. Fortunately or unfortunately, depending on a person's view, he ended up in the basement, the victim of a trap door. The bartender thereupon jettisoned the booze in his absence.

Supposedly the old safe here held deposit boxes where patrons kept a private bottle as well, it being illegal to search a safe deposit box without a warrant. If Prohibition produced nothing else, it produced stories.

The Balboa Cafe was a man's saloon for most of its history; the old photos of a no-nonsense stand-up bar and pool tables attest to that. Opened in 1914 under its present name, it goes back further as a saloon, and still further as a meat market. The saloon may have begun in 1896; a city water permit for two horse troughs bears that date.

With its restored interior of brass, velvet and gilt-gold mirror, and daily papers hanging on a rack, the Balboa still seems a throwback to an earlier time. The old Wurlitzer jukebox is art deco at its finest, and other mementos draw the eye.

A lot is different here from the turn of the century, when the location was almost countryside and the shore was within a couple of blocks. Class comes with history, and the Balboa has it.

3199 Fillmore Street, 921-3944

Perry's

CHARLES McCABE, San Francisco columnist and high priest of its saloons, once ordained Perry's "Mr. Perry Butler's seminary for drinkers." He wasn't far off.

Since opening its door slightly more than a decade ago, it has been Union Street distilled down to one saloon. It is a stylish, modern pub with more than a tinge of New York to it, where the etiquette of social drinking has been elevated to an art. Aspiring students have given nighttime Perry's the unwanted image of a den for chic singles, but such is Union Street. Regulars who know the true character of the place tolerate them, if a bit grumpily. A wide variety of San Francisco luminaries enliven the place.

Every element of Perry's bears the stamp of meticulous care. Butler's fine eye for entertaining photographs, prints and tracts from writers make his saloon a virtual gallery of memorabilia. Everything from a plethora of great-moments-in-sports photos to movie posters grace the walls; even the autographed picture of Hopalong Cassidy fits into the montage.

The staff consists of a few highly literate and understanding artisans of their trades, some of whom work here entirely by choice. One bartender, for instance, is an accomplished tuba player and member of the Bohemian Club as well. All of them insure civility is maintained.

A bright place of wood and tile and checkered tablecloths, Perry's serves up a generous slice of the Big Apple on Union Street, rolling a haven for the Izod generation and a genteel neighborhood bar into one drinking establishment.

1944 Union Street, 922-9022

106 • *Union/Chestnut/Polk*

Henry Africa's

*"Life is just a joke to him
He was never meant to win.
He's a rolling stone, it's bred in the bone,
He's a man who can't fit in."*

From "The Saga of Henry Africa," 1ère Coloniale Parachutiste

REALITY PLAYS ABOUT as large a part in Norm Hobday's saloons as in his attitude toward life. Fact and fancy constantly butt heads in both. A lot of people have tried to copy Henry Africa's and failed because, as Hobday will gladly tell you, "Sir, that whole bar is me."

A fascinating, if slightly frightening thought. Walking into Henry Africa's is like walking straight into Norm Hobday's childhood fantasies. If F.A.O. Schwartz got into the saloon business, it could do no better.

The decor is pure Willie Wonka. While a tuxedoed piano player pounds out all manner of tunes from a mirrored alcove overhead, electric trains race around the walls on elevated tracks. The Tiffany lamps are original, as are the two classic motorcycles hanging in the window and the two stained glass windows, "Sunrise" and "Sunset," plucked from the crypt of Harry Houdini.

The bar is the original from Denver's Brown Palace Hotel, where such Old West stalwarts as Annie Oakley, George Custer, Teddy Roosevelt and Buffalo Bill once drank. Oh, if they knew where their bar was now.

As a bar, Henry Africa's breaks all the rules and wins. Everything, but everything, there has a story, true or not, courtesy of Norm Hobday's rambling sense of American history. After all, maybe Henry Africa was right, maybe life *is* just a joke.

2260 Van Ness Avenue, 928-7044

Buzzby's

IT WAS ONCE, not so many years ago, the lone disco on Polk Street, the first and foremost in flash fever for the neighborhood gay crowd. Word of mouth brought people from all over the world to Buzzby's. The wait to get in sometimes took hours, the doorman doubling as arbiter of who got in and who didn't. With the driving beat of its dance tunes and its pulsing aura of psychedelia gone disco, Buzzby's was the king of good times on Polk.

Busby Berkeley's namesake has done him proud, with a medley of flashing red and aquamarine lights and a nearly carnival atmosphere. Inside Buzzby's feels like being inside a three-dimensional cartoon show looking out. It's been redecorated three times, with stuffed clowns on trapezes swinging overhead, cradling mirrored globes in their laps, and stuffed animals in circus cages gracing the place.

Corn meal covers the dancefloor of polished steel, and DJs orchestrate tunes from an overhead booth. Like most serious partying and dance bars, any furnishings within reach are basically utilitarian and unbreakable.

The burgeoning of competitors in past years has thinned the crowd at Buzzby's somewhat. Now there's a sadness behind Buzzby's as faint as the sadness behind a fixed smile. After nearly a decade, the flash may not be quite as bright, but behind the art deco exterior, disco still rules.

1436 Polk Street, 474-4246

Hotel Utah

SCRATCH THE SURFACE of the Hotel Utah, and Big Al's Trans Bay Tavern shows through. Big Al is Al Opatz, who from 1946 until 1978 ran a battleship-gray-on-the-outside, blue-collar-on-the-inside saloon in the warehouse district south of Mission.

The Trans Bay was born with the bridge it was named for, and virtually in its shadow. It was a haven for the working-men of the district whose livelihood came and went with the industry.

As small as it was crowded, Big Al's made a name for itself. Joe Dimaggio and Marilyn Monroe frequented the place, and the first well of the backbar is still a shrine to her. Newspapermen were regulars as well, with Herb Caen and Charles McCabe turning their saloon-trained pens on it. Even Dirty Harry got into the act when he uttered "You can get me at Al's Trans Bay."

Then, in 1978, screenwriter Paul Gaer took over, buying the bar with the proceeds of his script for "The Electric Horseman." He brought back the original name of the building, calling it the Hotel Utah, added a rollicking cabaret for a myriad of acts, repainted the exterior bright colors and, in general, added a fanciful layer of chic to a fading warehouse district tavern. He did, however, keep one thing. He did manage to keep Al on as bartender, who loved the place too much to leave altogether.

The result is a mingling of old timers from Al's and a young crowd drawn by the cabaret. The rejuvenation created a genuine people's bar: Destination signs from the marquees of buses serve as curtains, giving the place an aura of a bus going everywhere and nowhere at the same time. The arching backbar was one of four made at the Fitchburg Breweries of Belgium in the 1850s, then brought around the Horn as part of a promotion. Back then, a saloon owner need only sign a several-year contract with a liquor supplier, and he got his bar gratis.

400 Fourth Street, 421-8308

Stud

ATE IN THE EVENING, when the crowd at the Stud begins to build in earnest, so does the electricity. It's as if some invisible director decreed "Let the good times roll," and roll they do. The dancing spills off the dancefloor and throughout the bar, people beating tambourines and maracas to the party music. Everyone seems permanently turned on in this roller coaster ride of a saloon.

Like a chameleon, the Stud has shifted its colors easily to suit the tides of public fashion throughout its fifteen-year sojourn on Folsom. Throw in varying portions of leather, three-piece suit, punk, disco, New Wave and gay, blend with a lot of high energy and good humor, and the Stud is the result.

Three years or so ago, it was an even wilder place. The punk rockers ruled in all their glory, bringing their belligerence along with their energy, slam-dancing their way into the hearts of each other. This was in fact the first place to bring new wave to the city, but things have since toned down a bit.

The barnwood interior is devoid of tables or barstools to slow people down. The floor came from an old church. Regulars and staff are always bringing in momentos for the walls: a wooden fireplace mantle hung upside-down, a piece of stained glass from the 1900s, pictures and statues of horses (the Stud, remember?) and other items. The train by the door was constructed by a former manager of the place at the expense of his roommate's cooking gear.

The best thing to ever happen to the Stud was the demise of the Universal Life Corral next door. After that, the common wall came down, instantly doubling the bar in size. All that remains of the former haven of flower power is its sign, hanging over the Stud's bar. One look at the eclectic crowd beneath it makes that sign seem far more appropriate where it is now.

1535 Folsom Street, 863-6623

Hamburger Mary's

IRECTLY OVER THE FRONT DOOR a sign exhorts passers-by to "Start your miracle at Mary's," and undoubtedly more than a few are giving it their best shot.

Mary's is Mary's. At its peak, you don't go to Hamburger Mary's so much as throw yourself at it. With the resonant pounding of the disco beat and a spirit of manic euphoria, it is high voltage saloonery, a foliage and antique jungle with all the order and decorum of a high speed auto chase.

Amid the parasols and antique lamps, the old paintings and models and everything else imaginable that obscure the barnboard walls is a liberal sampling of all God's known human creations. Gay, punk, New Wave, straight and three-piece suit rub shoulders, with an occasional construction worker thrown in to confuse the casual observer. Nobody, but nobody, looks incongruous.

Mary's is a place where an old painting of a mother and children in an ornate gold gilt frame becomes comic, while a life preserver inscribed "Titanic" may just be real. An old wagon becomes a planter box. A purloined sign nailed on the wall that offers a reward for "the capture of anyone defacing this property" looks like an after-the-fact posting. As artfully done as it is, the place looks like your great aunt's garage sale waiting to happen.

Barely controlled confusion isn't a constant by any means, casual Sunday brunches prove that. But the more crowded it

gets, the crazier it gets. Mary's may just be the bar of the 80s, where the accent is on a maximum of energy and a minimum of rules.

1582 Folsom Street, 626-5767

Swede's

ONE OLDER GENTLEMAN at the bar, a victim of bourbon and circumstances, was talking about dreams; about how they seem to be just a little harder to cling to these days, how somewhere along the line getting rich had lost out to just getting by. He allowed as to it didn't make him sad exactly. But live in the Mission District all your life, live a long life and a lot of change happens anyway.

Swede's has been in the Mission all his life, but not much is different now about it. Everybody at the bar agreed. Not that it ever was much to look at. Layers of cigarette smoke have clouded the front window to the point it's no longer transparent. And the bar has been decorated in that haphazard fashion where arcane items find their way onto the walls, but for some reason or another don't find their way off again. If the old backbar came around the Horn, nobody knows, or even cares. The chief relic is the carcass of a pinball machine.

The regulars, which accounts for pretty much everyone at Swede's, all know each other's business, never hesitating to offer each other advice, wanted or not. They are often retired, good-hearted men, short on money and long on dignity. They come to drink and be together, to play cribbage or rummy and pass the time away among familiar and trusted faces. What counts is that they watch out for each other.

Now, like many little bars, Swede's is threatened by rent increases and hard times, to the point where Florence and Swede may just decide to retire. For the people who frequent those bars, who depend on them for companionship, it will be a hard loss; yet another step in the letting go of dreams.

3200 16th Street, 626-6804